Other *Handing on the Faith* titles:

Your Child's Baptism

Your Child's First Penance

Your Child's Confirmation

First Communion
R E C O R D

_____

Child's Name

_____

Parents

_____

Date of First Communion

_____

Priest

_____

Church

_____

Address

_____

City, State

Your Child's First Communion

Carol Luebering

ST. ANTHONY MESSENGER PRESS
Cincinnati, Ohio

Nihil Obstat
Rev. Lawrence Landini, O.F.M.
Rev. Edward J. Gratsch

Imprimi Potest
Rev. Fred Link, O.F.M.
Provincial

Imprimatur
+Most Rev. Carl K. Moeddel
Vicar General and Auxiliary Bishop
Archdiocese of Cincinnati
February 22, 2000

The *nihil obstat* and *imprimatur* are a declaration that a book or pamphlet is considered to be free from doctrinal or moral error. It is not implied that those who have granted the *nihil obstat* and *imprimatur* agree with the contents, opinions or statements expressed.

Scripture citations are taken from *New Revised Standard Version* of the Bible, copyright ©1989 by the Division of Christian Education of the National Council of Churches of Christ in the U.S.A., and used by permission. All rights reserved.

Excerpts from the English translation of *The Roman Missal*, copyright ©1973, International Committee on English in the Liturgy, Inc. (ICEL); from the English translation of *Eucharistic Prayers for Masses With Children*, copyright ©1975, ICEL; from the English translation of *Eucharistic Prayers for Masses of Reconciliation*, copyright ©1975, ICEL, are reprinted with permission. All rights reserved.

Cover and interior illustrations by Julie Lonneman
Cover and book design by Mary Alfieri

ISBN 0-86716-344-5

Copyright ©2000, Carol Luebering
All rights reserved.

Published by St. Anthony Messenger Press
www.AmericanCatholic.org
Printed in the U.S.A.

Contents

Introduction 1

A Place at the Table 5

A Family Meal 11

The Lord's Supper 17

The Table of Sacrifice . . 23

Table Customs 29

Notes 33

Introduction

When you presented your child for Baptism, the priest or deacon asked you, "What do you ask of God's Church for (name)?" You probably answered with a single word that contained your hopes and dreams for your child: something like *faith*, *life*, *Baptism*.

No one will ask you to state your expectations on your child's First Communion day. Now it is your youngster's turn to make a one-word response—to speak an amen, an assent in faith, to a statement overlaid with many levels of meaning: "The Body of Christ."

But the loving web of hopes and fears you began to weave around your child before you saw his face do not dissolve when he reaches the age of seven—or seventeen or twenty-seven. As your child prepares to receive Eucharist for the first time, you are surrounding that day with your own dreams. And that is as it should be, for your parenthood reflects the parenthood of the God Jesus called Father. Eucharist, believers insist, expresses God's dream for all human children.

Memories of your own First Communion with all its

promise and excitement (and, perhaps, disappointments), your experience at the Lord's table over the years since that day, your hopes for your child's future relationship to God, your faith and your doubts—all these are the stuff of which your dreams are made.

Other dreams spun by family members, catechists and classmates, your parish staff and your parish community also surround your youngster, for Eucharist is the focus of all believers' dreams. It is, in believing minds, intimately connected with the deepest aspirations of the human heart. It speaks many aspects of our hunger for God: meal, sacrifice, initiation, unity.

'To Give Thanks'

The word *eucharist* comes from a Greek word meaning "to give thanks." It refers not only to the bread and wine, the Body and Blood of Christ, but also to what believers do at Mass: give thanks to God through Jesus, who is Lord.

At the center of all those dreams stands your child, a small person who is developing certain expectations of her own. But your child's dreams of First Communion will be shaped primarily by the understanding significant adults bring to the day. Should your youngster feel tension between your expectations and those of other grownups, her approach to the Lord's table will be at least slightly soured, and the day will disappoint everyone.

Your Child's First Communion will help you explore the many levels of meaning Christians celebrate in Eucharist, to deepen your understanding of what you and others hope for your child's First Communion day. It includes background thoughts on your experience as a parent and quotations from Scripture, the liturgy of the sacrament and the *Catechism of the Catholic Church* to ponder, as well as questions to guide your reflection and discussion.

A Place at the Table

Just a few years ago your child made a momentous move: from high chair to the table. The high chair tray was a safety net for the failings of spoon and finger acrobatics. And, when you failed to notice an eager toddler, spoon or cup served as gavel. A child enthroned in a high chair demands the center of attention.

And then one day you placed a chair at the table for your youngster. It was an adventure in growing up, certain proof of having attained "big boy" or "big girl" status. For you it was an adventure of a different sort: You set your table afloat on the uncharted sea of family meals. (Literally afloat—how much spilled milk has cascaded across it?)

Being at the helm of that unseaworthy barge is a chore. Making mealtime a pleasant experience means a constant war against impossible table manners, sibling rivalry and menu disapproval, interruptive or inappropriate conversation, the lure of TV and waiting playmates. And sometimes you wonder if it's worth the effort.

It is, even if you only try occasionally. A family meal

provides more than physical nourishment. It speaks of sharing resources, emotional involvement and mutual dependence. Family members rediscover and celebrate their relationship to one another at the table.

The baby in the high chair shares the warmth of that gathering, but the people who sit at the table create the atmosphere. Your child's sense of bigness at coming to the table was right on the mark: The move to the table is the beginning of more active participation in the reality of family.

That participation is marked by privileges. A child at the table shares the same food the rest of the family eats (even though someone may have to help with a knife) and takes part in the dinner-table conversation.

It is also a time of new responsibilities: no more eating with fingers, no more banging for attention, no more unchallenged right to the center of attention. Children who sit at the table are expected to contribute, within the limits of their ability, to the well-being of the whole family.

The baby you presented for Baptism was a wholly self-centered individual who accepted welcome into the Church family without notice. Babies are more concerned about empty tummies or diaper discomfort than about God's invitation to eternal life. On that day, you spoke for your infant out of your hopes and dreams for the child. And the gathered community accepted your word and welcomed the baby in your arms as a member of the family we call Church.

Baptism brought your child into the Church family as irrevocably as birth or adoption forged a bond with you. This child is your son or daughter forever. Just so, he or she has a lasting right to address other Christians as family. Baptism is indeed a birth.

But birth is only a beginning. Full participation in a family comes with growth. Just as the move from high chair to table represented a new stage in your child's growth as a family member, so First Communion marks a new stage in your child's relationship to the Christian community, another step in the initiation process that began with Baptism and includes Confirmation.

Age for First Communion

A century ago, children received Confirmation and First Communion when they were nearly adults by the standards of their society—teens already contributing fully to the family's welfare and nearly ready for marriage. The eucharistic meal was a formal affair from which small children were excluded until Pope Pius X, feeling that small children belonged at the Lord's table, lowered the age for First Communion in 1910.

In the beginning you nurtured the baptismal gift of faith in the same way you nourished your baby's tiny body: with the warmth of your arms and the tenderness in your voice. Cuddling and crooning gave more than the assurance of your love. You laid the foundations of belief in a loving God who made the world good.

As your child grew, so did faith, nurtured by the prayers you taught and shared, the wonderful discoveries you made together in the world of creation, your attempts to explain the magnitude of God in terms a child's mind could grasp. You gave your little one a "high chair" view of Sunday worship, an opportunity to absorb the sights and smells and sounds of God's people gathered for Eucharist. The shushing finger on your lips clearly conveyed that something important was happening here, that whatever was being dispensed from those shiny dishes must be very special indeed.

Your child has outgrown the high chair and passed beyond the secure limits of your family to become a member of the wider community. No more are your arms the only security. Your youngster is learning to function in at least one corner of the world outside your door—the classroom—and has begun to speak a personal expression of the baptismal faith, combining what you have taught with the perceptions of teachers and friends.

And so your child is ready to join the larger family we call Church at the table where this family discovers and celebrates its identity.

For Reflection and Discussion

- What do you remember of family meals in your childhood?
- What makes your family mealtime memorable?
- What would help to make mealtime more meaningful?
- How does the Eucharist help you experience your parish as family?

Father, hear the prayers of the family you have gathered here before you. In mercy and love unite all your children wherever they may be. (Eucharistic Prayer III)

For this reason I bow my knees before the Father, from whom every family in heaven and on earth takes its name. I pray that, according to the riches of his glory, he may grant that you may be strengthened in your inner being with power through his Spirit, and that Christ may dwell in your hearts through faith, as you are being rooted and grounded in love. I pray that you may have the power to comprehend, with all the saints, what is the breadth and length and height and depth, and to know the love of Christ that surpasses knowledge, so that you may be filled with all the fullness of God. (Ephesians 3:14-19)

Parents have the first responsibility for the education of their children. They bear witness to this responsibility first by *creating a home* where tenderness, forgiveness, respect, fidelity, and disinterested service are the rule.... The home is the natural environment for initiating a human being into solidarity and communal responsibilities. (*Catechism of the Catholic Church*, #2223-2224)

A Family Meal

All over the world, families sit down to eat at the end of the day. The menu varies: Middle-class Americans may enjoy bread made from Kansas wheat, beef raised in Australia, vegetables grown in the Southwest or in Florida, coffee imported from the Brazilian mountains and tea from Asia. An African family on the edge of the Sahara may have a little grain boiled in precious drops of dew that children gathered in the early morning before the greedy sun devoured all moisture.

However rich or poor the fare, it belongs to all who gather at the table. Those who earn or prepare food have no greater claim than the smallest child, the frail elder, the sickest or most handicapped member of the family. The whole family has an unquestionable right to share the family meal.

Sharing a meal is unknown in the rest of the animal kingdom. A pride of lions may dine on the same carcass, but with thinly disguised tolerance and frequent snarls. Nesting birds will bring food to the young, but once the brood is grown, it's every bird for itself again. Only human beings freely choose to share the daily diet with one another. Every time you call your child to the table, you affirm your unique place in God's creation.

Uniquely human, too, is the ability to make meals special. On Thanksgiving Day people prepare an extraordinary feast and invite aunts and uncles and cousins, grandparents and close friends, perhaps even a stranger who has nowhere to go. That meal is so special it redefines the limits of family.

A child soon begins to understand that this holiday meal celebrates the fulfillment of an old dream spun by a people who faced great hardship. By now your child can retell the story of the Pilgrims' grand feast with their native advisers. Your child is beginning to understand that Thanksgiving commemorates the beginning of a new family identity and celebrates membership in one particular national family.

The people of Israel—Jesus' larger family—also celebrated a meal that recalled the beginning of a new national identity. Four thousand years ago a scattering of Semites living in Egypt were pressed into service of the pharaoh's building plans. One memorable night those slaves prepared a meal of roasted lamb and unleavened bread, and waited to see if a man named Moses could deliver promised freedom while their oppressors mourned the death of the firstborn in every household.

That night they escaped Egypt and began a long, hard journey to the Promised Land. Along the way they gained a sense of themselves as a people, a family of families bound by one experience. And their descendants especially remembered one stop in the journey at the foot of a mountain called Sinai, where they discovered that something more bound them together. As the mountain shuddered, a mighty voice handed down the "house rules"—the Ten Commandments—and the God of Israel adopted the band of fugitives as family.

Jews still celebrate their flight from Egypt to freedom and their adoption as God's special people in the Passover meal. The youngest child asks the meaning of this family gathering: "Why is this night different from any other?" And the family retells its history, just as American families recall the Pilgrims' flight from the Old World to freedom in the New.

Christian tradition situates the Last Supper in the Passover tradition. Three evangelists identify the event in the Upper Room as a Passover observance; only John places it a day earlier. The Gospels agree on one thing: The death and resurrection of Jesus Christ is the New Passover, the event by which Jesus and the family he has gathered pass from slavery to freedom, from the bondage of sin and death to everlasting life.

The first Christians recalled their adoption as God's privileged children in a way that was both similar and quite new. They celebrated their unity with the beloved Son, in a new way—the Eucharist. They did what Jesus commanded at the Last Supper: blessing the broken bread and wine outpoured and partaking in his body and blood "in memory of me." Like Passover, Eucharist recalls God's saving action on the first Easter weekend in a family meal.

Eucharist and Sunday

The first Christians still considered themselves Jews. They went to the synagogue to pray and hear Scripture in a ritual akin to our Liturgy of the Word. They celebrated Eucharist in someone's home. It included a potluck supper with others who had become part of the family by virtue of their common belief in Jesus. Sunday, the day of the Resurrection, soon became the day they gathered.

As the family grew, new places were set at the Lord's table. First Communion was not a separate celebration then. Baptism, Confirmation and Eucharist were a single gesture of welcome to new believers.

Like all families, the Church changed with the years. New customs grew up in response to changing times; old traditions lay forgotten. The sacraments of initiation became separate moments.

Parents still brought their infants for Baptism, eager to share the gift of eternal life. But the sealing and nourishment of that life—Confirmation and Eucharist—were postponed until the child had grown into the family identity.

When storms rage outside, families huddle a little closer together. Perhaps it is only natural that, in a world swept by technological change, the family we call Church seeks renewed intimacy at the family table. But where would family intimacy be without the children?

Your child is now old enough to ask how this meal is different from every other, to listen as the elders retell the story of Jesus' death and resurrection. Your child has begun to sense that he is part of a unique family. And, as part of the family, your youngster has a right to join us at the family table.

For Reflection and Discussion

- *How do the meals you share with people beyond your household nurture a sense of belonging to a wider family? (Consider Christmas and Thanksgiving celebrations, Fourth of July picnics, other extended family gatherings.)*

- *With what feelings does your child anticipate these events?*

- *Does the Church have the feeling of home to you? Why or why not? How has that sense developed since your own First Communion?*

- *What feeling of home do you want the Church to have for your child? How do you hope First Communion will begin to build that sense of belonging?*

We thank you above all for your Son,
   Jesus Christ....
He opened our eyes and our hearts
to understand that we are brothers and
   sisters,
and that you are Father of us all.
He now brings us together to one table
and asks us to do what he did.

(Eucharistic Prayer for Children III)

Day by day, as they spent much time together in the temple, they broke bread at home and ate their food with glad and generous hearts, praising God and having the goodwill of all the people. And day by day the Lord added to their number those who were being saved. (Acts 2:46-47)

By celebrating the Last Supper with his apostles in the course of the Passover meal, Jesus gave the Jewish Passover its definitive meaning. Jesus' passing over to his father by his death and Resurrection, the new Passover, is anticipated in the Supper and celebrated in the Eucharist.... (*Catechism of the Catholic Church,* #1340)

The Lord's Supper

Grain simmered in scarce water and a meal chosen from supermarket variety are both center and symbol of family unity. But the child whose family scrapes a bare existence has only a slim chance of long and healthy life.

Your child has enjoyed the best diet you can afford. However tight your budget, your youngster had the privilege of taking a dislike to peas or beets or spinach as you teased taste buds with a variety of foods. Meats and milk products, grains, fruits and vegetables—a balance of earth's gifts has endowed your youngster with sturdy muscles and an energy level that outruns yours.

Maintaining that balance is not easy. You urge some foods and restrict others. Cookies and candy and soft drinks may well be your offspring's preference, but your concern is healthy growth.

Youngsters grow in more than body. Concern for your child's development in faith prompted your decision to present your infant for Baptism. You hoped that living in the Church family would help to heal the inborn wound of selfishness and implant in your child a hunger for goodness.

In welcoming your child to its family table, the Church reflects your longstanding concern for your child's nutrition. Here there is no junk food, only a taste of bread and wine.

Eucharist as Meal

As the Christian community grew and moved into large public buildings for worship, the celebration of Eucharist at a meal ended. Increasingly awed by the presence of the divine Lord, many people hesitated to receive Communion. From the Middle Ages into the twentieth century, Eucharist was less a family meal than something the clergy did while the people watched in adoration.

This is not ordinary food. At the Lord's table, an entirely new element is introduced into your chid's diet. The Bread of Life—that is what Jesus himself called his self-gift. He offers food that builds not strong bones and sturdy muscles, but a vitality of mind and heart and spirit death cannot destroy—his own body and blood.

Old-timers at the Lord's table bring with them a

sense of the meal honed by long experience. There they have known moments of deep and real intimacy; they can also recall moments when the food tasted flat and family quarrels spoiled the atmosphere.

If you could, you would erase from your child's memory all traces of tension around your table and rejoice in the certainty that she would grow up remembering only love. The family that is Church has the same wish. Perhaps that is why countless generations of children have been told that their First Communion day should be a day of great happiness.

But relationships, like healthy bodies, are nourished best when the diet is varied. Your child will carry a sense of family through life because your table is an expression of love's power to endure in spite of everything. Your youngster will not forget the day you overreacted to a milk spill or the evening an unresolved quarrel weighted the table with silence.

Nor should those moments be erased from your history. Balanced by the good times, they are the spinach and liver of your family's diet: perhaps not tasty, but still nurturing growth. For your child is learning at your table that clumsiness and misunderstanding and disagreement matter less than acceptance and forgiveness and love. The lesson is not learned at a single meal, but discovered over years of experience.

The family that gathers at the Lord's table is as unruly as any other. Most of its members manage to be wise and loving and forgiving only sometimes. That, of course, is why they come to the Lord's table for nourishment. Like children whose growing bodies need extra protein and calcium, believers come to the Lord's table because they are still hungry for goodness and forgiveness. And the patient Lord continues to give as food his boundless mercy and love.

In the world of fantasy, food has an instant effect. Popeye's muscles swell with a can of spinach; Alice nibbles her way through Wonderland, altering her size in seconds.

In real life, nourishment is a slower process. The glass of orange juice your child drank this morning will not provide tomorrow's vitamin C; a shipment of powdered milk to a drought-stricken corner of Africa may not reverse lifelong malnourishment. Just so, the life of the risen Lord is best nurtured by a lifetime diet of his Body and Blood. Your child's First Communion is but the first taste.

Remember your child's delight at the magical first taste of ice cream? The first taste of Eucharist may be much less pleasing to the mouth. The meal the Lord offers is simple; the portions are scanty. The sweetness of Eucharist stems from our union with the Lord and one another.

Relationships, too, have magical moments, and the first step to new intimacy is often counted among them. But real intimacy unfolds before you gradually through the years, and there are always new discoveries waiting.

Your child's First Communion is a step into new intimacy with the Lord. From Baptism, your child has been one with Jesus, filled with his indestructible life. Eucharist marks a new stage in the relationship with Christ, as physical as making love to a spouse or embracing a child.

And it is, like marriage or parenthood, an intimacy

which unfolds over a lifetime. Only when your child has grown well into adulthood will you grasp the full import of the adventure begun when you held an infant in your arms for the first time. And one day, belief holds, at the end of life's journey, we will come to a table laden with a rich feast and surrounded by a family forgiven, forgiving and bound in enduring love. There, at last, in the host's welcoming embrace, the intimacy nourished by Eucharist will become everlasting unity with God and with one another.

For Reflection and Discussion

- *How has your understanding of parenthood changed since the arrival of your child? How are the members of your family dearer today than when your relationship first began?*

- *What impressions of your First Communion can you recall?*

- *How has Eucharist nourished you as a person? How has it nourished your relationship with God? With others?*

- *What do you hope Eucharist will nourish in your child? What do you hope his or her first reception of Eucharist will be like?*

Fill us with his Spirit
through our sharing in this meal.
May he take away all that divides us....
In that new world where the fullness
    of your peace will be revealed,
gather people of every race, language,
    and way of life
to share in the one eternal banquet
with Jesus Christ the Lord.

    (Eucharistic Prayer for Masses of
    Reconciliation II)

"I am the living bread that came down from heaven. Whoever eats of this bread will live forever; and the bread that I will give for the life of the world is my flesh." (John 6:51)

Thus from celebration to celebration, as they proclaim the Paschal mystery of Jesus "until he comes," the pilgrim People of God advances, "following the narrow way of the cross," toward the heavenly banquet, when all the elect will be seated at the table of the kingdom. (*Catechism of the Catholic Church*, #1344)

The Table of Sacrifice

No food appears on the family table without cost. It takes time and labor to provide and prepare food. The family meal always contains an element of sacrifice, a gift of love freely given.

You quickly discovered that parenthood means sacrifice. Your child cries out in the night, and you respond—even when the day has been long and trying, and you crave rest. But that is your way of life as a parent. Your life—personal, social, economic—has been reshaped around the needs of your child.

Whatever resentment may surface from time to time, you would not have it any other way. You can barely distinguish between your needs and the child's. The sacrifices you make are expressions of the unity between you and your child.

Christians speak of God as a parent. Jesus addressed God with an intimate title: *Abba*, Father. The history of God's relationship with humanity is parental: attentive, tender, disciplining, patiently explaining. From the beginning, God has yearned for intimacy with humankind.

When humans refused the divine invitation to loving unity, God made an extraordinary move—into the world of human pain. And a child was born in an insignificant Middle Eastern village, a child who was the perfect unity of humanity and divinity: Jesus of Nazareth.

That child learned and grew and developed as all human children must. He learned a sense of family at the table in his parents' home. He learned of his larger family, celebrating Israel's history in the Passover meal. He listened for God's whispers in the Scriptures and sensed God's dream for the whole human family.

What he learned, he lived. The grown-up Jesus left the security of the Nazareth home for the highways and byways of Israel. Wherever he walked, he offered love to the unlovable, forgiveness to the sinful, healing to the suffering and friendship even to the enemy. Always, there was a price attached. He knew heat and thirst and weariness. Crowds pressed him when he wanted a little time alone with his friends. He knew the pain of having his love refused, the disapproval of Israel's leadership and misunderstanding from his closest companions.

He became too great a threat to those who believed sacrifice should be measurable by regulations. Because many religious leaders thought him too careless in his definition of family, he headed for death at the hands of his own.

The night before his death, he sat at table with the family he had gathered. He gave them bread and wine, saying it was his body about to be broken, his blood about to be poured out. In that action he asserted his willingness to sacrifice his life as a sign of the unity between God and humanity. At the Last Supper, Jesus offered his life in a gesture that captured the meaning of the next day's events.

A few days later Jesus stood again with his friends. The earth welcomed the footprints of one who was all the Creator had planned for all of us: human flesh endowed with lasting life. Jesus Christ freely gave his life to express the unity between God and us. Wherever we meet the risen Lord, we meet the crucified Jesus.

For Christians, that encounter is most unmistakable in the gesture Jesus used to express himself: broken bread and outpoured wine. The child you bring to his table stands with all believers at the foot of the cross.

The Nature of Eucharist

In the wake of Reformation arguments over the nature of Eucharist, Catholic stress fell on the sacrificial aspect. The Mass, we believe, draws back the curtain of time and transports us back to Calvary. But this emphasis on "the Holy Sacrifice of the Mass" also lessened Catholics' sense of the Eucharist as a meal until the reforms of Vatican II.

Your child has little sense of the sacrifices you have made on his behalf. Nevertheless, your sacrifices are woven into your child's history, your child's very being. He has absorbed your generosity from unconscious infancy.

Jesus' sacrifice has also been part of your child's story from Baptism. The love God spoke in Jesus is woven through your little one's life. Her generous impulses reflect not only your love, but also the love whose ultimate expression was a death on Calvary.

Every believer's life unfolds in that context. Because Jesus died for us, we are able, in small ways and sometimes in large ones, to die for one another. In Catholic belief, Jesus' sacrifice and our own have become one. The sacrifice of sleep to a child's need, sacrifices to any other person's needs become one sacrifice offered in love and faith with Jesus'.

Your child does not yet understand. It is all a young person can do to share toys with siblings or play quietly when a parent has a headache; the total surrender of a life is beyond the grasp of a child's imagination.

But neither have most adults fully grasped the meaning of the cross. Most of us struggle daily against the pull to achieve comfort, security and happiness. The sacrifices we gladly make for others reflect unity only within small circles of family and friendship. We still draw lines against those who are different or unknown; we still pass the judgments Jesus warned us against, pinning nasty labels on other members of the human family. We are far from the unity with God and all humanity expressed in Jesus' sacrifice.

At every Eucharist we admit our failings. We ask the Lord's mercy, and we turn to our neighbors in the pews to express the unity we crave with a sign of peace.

Your child's First Communion will not create the

perfection toward which we all journey. More than one first communicant, disappointed in the day which was supposed to be the happiest, has arrived at sundown in a magnificent pout—just as many an adult communicant has ended the day with an unloving action.

None of us has yet had our fill at the Lord's table. But we trust that his nourishment will yet bring us to perfect union with God and with one another.

For Reflection and Discussion

- *What are some of the sacrifices your child has already cost you? What sacrifices can you foresee in the years to come? Admit the burdens and ask yourself if you really regret what you must give.*

- *What sacrifices have you made in regard to your parish family, or the larger family of God in your local community, or the world?*

- *What growth in willingness to sacrifice have you seen in your child? What growth do you yet hope to see?*

- *What meaning does the cross express for you? What meaning do you want it to have for your child?*

From age to age you gather a
 people to yourself,
so that from east to west
a perfect offering may be made
to the glory of your name.
 (Eucharistic Prayer III)

Then he took a loaf of bread, and when he had given thanks, he broke it and gave it to them, saying, "This is my body, which is given for you. Do this in remembrance of me." And he did the same with the cup after supper, saying, "This cup that is poured out for you is the new covenant in my blood, shed for you." (Luke 22:19-20)

In the Eucharist Christ gives us the very body which he gave up for us on the cross, the very blood which he "poured out for many for the forgiveness of sins."
(*Catechism of the Catholic Church*, #1365)

Table Customs

We use symbols and gestures—ritual—to express realities that elude words. Your child mastered that language long ago, learning to smile, to hug, to sit as part of the family at the table. And children are natural ritual-makers. Family traditions are born when a child insists that "we always do it this way."

Eucharist expresses Jesus' presence in ways words can only dimly echo: He is the sacrifice we offer, nourishing food, source of our unity with God and with one another.

Your child has never made a First Communion before. A variety of expectations and understandings of Eucharist are all converging on one small person. Work out with your child how you will celebrate the day.

Eucharist is a family celebration—our immediate family, the parish family and the universal Church. Some parishes allow the choice of receiving Eucharist for the first time at the parish Sunday celebration or with the whole First Communion class, and arguments can be advanced for either.

Other parishes dictate the choice, and it may not fit either your fondest wishes or your child's. If the First Communion were the last, surrendering your dreams for the day to someone else's would be painful. But if you see it as only the beginning of a life centered around the Eucharist, you can focus on your child's many family circles and find ways to make the first celebration with each of them special.

You will want to plan some celebration just for your immediate family for (and with) the newcomer to the Lord's table. If grandparents, godparents and other relatives particularly dear to your child are unable to be present for First Communion, try to join them at their parish family table in the near future.

The closest relationships your child enjoys with the parish family is with classmates. They will probably share Eucharist together many times in the years ahead, but you may want to emphasize the adventure they have embarked upon together by providing an opportunity for your child to receive Eucharist with at least a few close friends, perhaps after a Saturday night sleep-over or before Sunday brunch.

The parish family is familiar to your child from Sunday Mass. But does your youngster have any sense of the universal Church? Don't wait for vacation to take you to another church; plan a visit to another parish or two. Consider especially your cathedral church or an ethnic parish to show your child how big this family is.

Your child took the momentous step from high chair to your family table in everyday clothes. No special dress is required at the Lord's table, either. He who praised the lilies of the field has little use for fancy clothes. But your family has its own dress codes for Sunday dinner at Grandma's, for holiday meals and for church—and for First Communion attire.

If new suits or white dresses and veils are important to you or to your parish family, fine. But if your daughter prefers red or your son hates ties, remember what the Lord had to say about what people wear. Read Matthew 6:28-30 before you come to a final decision. In any case, your child's First Communion clothes announce to the parish community a new member at the family table. Encourage wearing them to church in the weeks after First Communion.

First Communion Clothes

In the early Church, people baptized during the Easter Vigil liturgy were immediately clothed in new white garments, which they wore throughout the Easter season. Getting new clothes for Easter reflects the same tradition. Even to longtime believers, the life won by Jesus is fresh and new each Easter season.

In countries where wine regularly appears on the family table, young children get a sip of watered wine. In most American families, wine is the mark of a very special occasion and lifting a glass is a privilege of adulthood.

Receiving only bread at Communion is enough. But bread and wine convey different meanings. Together they speak all the Lord is to us. He is our daily nourishment, the wheat of divine life ground fine for us. He is also the bubbling of joy in our lives and ease for all our sorrows—the twin poles of human existence to which people lift a glass of wine.

Whatever illusions parents hold about the innocence of childhood are likely to crumble on overhearing two first communicants in conversation: "I got $20; what did you get?" You can't always dictate what others will give your child, but you can see that your own gifts point to a future of loving unity with the Lord. A book of prayers or a children's Bible does more to support the nourishment of Eucharist than a new bicycle; a gift of money might be matched with a donation which will help to feed hungry children or heal sick ones.

In any case, your child's self-centeredness is not unusual. Your child is only a newcomer to the Lord's table; he or she has years to learn there the sharing in love you began to teach at your family table.

Notes